PARAGUAY

MAJOR WORLD NATIONS

PARAGUAY

Marion Morrison

CHELSEA HOUSE PUBLISHERS
Philadelphia

Chelsea House Publishers

Copyright © 2000 by Chelsea House Publishers,
a division of Main Line Book Co.
All rights reserved.
Printed in Malaysia

First Printing.

1 3 5 7 9 8 6 4 2

Library of Congress Cataloging-in-Publication Data

Morrison, Marion.
Paraguay / Marion Morrison.
p.   cm. — (Major world nations)
Includes index.
Summary: An overview of the history, geography, economy, government,
people, and culture of the South American country known as "the place
with the great river."
ISBN 0-7910-5393-8 (hc.)
1. Paraguay—Juvenile literature. [1. Paraguay.] I. Title.
II. Series.
F2668.5.M69   1999
989.2—dc21   99-13779
CIP

ACKNOWLEDGEMENTS

All illustrations in this book are the copyright of Marion and Tony Morrison/
South American Pictures

CONTENTS

FACTS AT A GLANCE

Land and People

Official Name Republic of Paraguay

Location Central South America, northeast of Argentina

Area 264,388 square miles (406,750 square kilometers)

Climate Subtropical

Capital Asunción

Other Cities Ciudad del Este, Concepción, Encarnación, San Lorenzo

Population 5,291,000

Population Distribution Urban, 50.3 percent; rural, 49.7 percent

Major Rivers Paraguay, Parana, Plate, Pilcomayo

Major Lakes Ypacarai

Highest Point Cerro San Rafael, 850 meters

Official Language Spanish

Other Languages Guarani, German

Religions	Roman Catholic, 90 percent; Mennonite and Protestant, 10 percent
Literacy Rate	92.1 percent
Average Life Expectancy	Males, 70.27 years; females, 74.29 years

Economy

Natural Resources	Water power, timber, limestone, iron ore, manganese
Agricultural Products	Cotton, sugarcane, soybean, corn, wheat, tobacco, fruits, coffee
Industries	Meat packing, textiles, construction, oilseed crushing, brewing
Major Imports	Consumer goods, food, raw materials, fuels
Major Exports	Cotton, soybeans, timber, meat, coffee
Major Trading Partners	Brazil, Netherlands, Argentina, United States, Uruguay, Chile
Currency	Guarani

Government

Form of Government	Republic
Government Bodies	Congress: Chamber of Senators, Chamber of Deputies
Formal Head of State	President

HISTORY AT A GLANCE

1524   A Portuguese explorer, Aleixo Garcia, sails up the Paraguay River and finds the Guarani tribe.

1537   Spanish settlers build a small fort and the town that develops around it is called Asunción. The area prospers as a farming community and relations with the Guarani are peaceful.

1588   Jesuits come into the area spreading the Christian religion.

early 17th century   Paraguay becomes a separate colony with its first governor, Hernando Arias de Saavedra (Hernandarias).

1609   The Jesuits build their first mission and encourage the Indians to live there under their protection allowing them to retain their tribal customs.

end of 17th century   Over 30 Jesuit missions are now in operation. The Jesuits educate over 100,000 Indians and teach them many skills.

1721   An attempt to overthrow the Spanish governor begins 15 years of struggle. The Portuguese in Brazil seize a large area of land in the north and it becomes a permanent part of Brazil.

9

1767	King Carlos III of Spain expels the Jesuits from the New World because they have become too powerful. The missions are eventually raided and destroyed and the Indians return to their homes.
1811	The neighboring Argentines send an army to try to subdue the Paraguayans but are met with fierce resistance. On May 11 Paraguay declares its independence from Spain.
1814-1840	José Gaspar Rodriguez de Francia (*El Supremo*) serves as the first president. He is a ruthless and brutal leader and closes all Paraguay's borders to the outside world.
1840s	Carlos Antonio Lopez becomes president. He modernizes the country—the transportation and communication networks are improved, docks and river forts built, the first railway laid, many schools built, and slavery abolished.
1853	Lopez sends his son, Francisco Solano Lopez, as an ambassador to Europe to gain knowledge from, and make alliances with, the outside world.
1862	Carlos Antonio Lopez dies and his son seizes power making himself president.
1864-1870	Uruguay, and Argentina join forces against Paraguay over border disputes and the use of the Plate River. The War of the Triple Alliance is fiercely and ruthlessly fought and devastates the country. Over half of the population is killed as is its president.
late 1800s	Following the war Paraguay is held by its three neighbors for over eight years. Political parties are formed and begin to come into power.

1904-1932	The Liberales Party leads the government for almost 30 years.
1932-1935	The Chaco War breaks out between Paraguay and Bolivia over ownership of the Chaco region. When a treaty is signed Paraguay keeps three-quarters of the region.
1935	After the war the peasants begin to demand better conditions. The Liberales Party president is deposed. Colonel Franco succeeds him and begins a period of social reform.
1939	The Liberales Party returns to power under Marshal Estigarribia. The social reforms continue until he is killed in a plane crash the next year.
1940-1948	General Morinigo becomes president at the death of Estigarribia. Money and technical assistance flow into the country from the United States because of the need for a strategic U.S. military base there during World War II. Morinigo takes advantage of the opportunities but rules with a brutal dictatorship.
1947	An unsuccessful revolt against Morinigo leaves thousands dead. The next year he is deposed by his own party.
1948-1954	Paraguay has six presidents in six years.
1954	The commander-in-chief of the armed forces, General Alfredo Stroessner becomes president.
1954-1989	Stroessner imposes a strict rule, harshly suppressing any dissent and exiling or imprisoning his opponents. He changes the constitution to allow himself to stand for reelection as many time as

11

desired. Some economic progress is made and the infrastructure improved.

1967   A new constitution allows a Congress to be elected by popular vote but Stroessner's Colorado Party continually dominates.

1988   Dissension rises in the Colorado Party toward Stroessner's methods.

1989   Stroessner is overthrown by a faction of his own party and goes into exile. General Andres Rodriguez becomes president.

1992   A new constitution is drafted incorporating democratic policies. Freedom of the press is restored, political parties reinstated, and political prisoners released.

1993   In the first free multiparty elections in Paraguay's history the Colorado Party candidate is elected. Juan Carlos Wasmosy becomes the first civilian president since 1954.

1995   Legislation is passed banning the military from joining political parties or participating in politics.

1997   In primary elections the Colorado Party bypasses Wasmosy's wishes and nominates a former general, Lino Oviedo.

1

"The Place with the Great River"

Paraguay is a small, little-known republic in the heart of South America. Hemmed in by its large, powerful neighbors, Brazil and Argentina, it is entirely landlocked, without any coastline, and with only one route by river to the sea. Traditionally a poor, agricultural country, it has only recently come to world attention by the creation of a huge hydroelectric dam–one of the largest in the world–on the Paraná River. The Itaipú Dam, as it is known, was built jointly by Paraguay and Brazil, as the Paraná River forms the border between the two countries, and it could transform backward Paraguay into an industrial nation of the future.

The Paraná River also forms the link between Paraguay and the outside world. The journey from the Atlantic coast and the Plate River to Asunción, the capital city of Paraguay, is about 1,000 miles (1,600 kilometers). For the first 800 miles (1,290 kilometers) the Paraná River runs north through Argentina. At the border with Paraguay, it is joined by its major tributary, the Paraguay

River. Asunción lies another 200 miles (320 kilometers) up the Paraguay River, at the confluence of the Paraguay and its tributary, the Pilcomayo. The Pilcomayo, which forms part of the frontier between Argentina and Paraguay, has its source in the Andes of Bolivia, to the northwest. From its junction with the Paraguay River, the Paraná River follows a course northeast to its source in the Brazilian Paraná Plateau. These two great rivers, the Paraguay and the Paraná, are the country's economic and trading lifeline. Oceangoing ships can make the journey from Buenos Aires in Argentina to Asunción in less than a week.

There are several explanations for the name Paraguay, and two, at least, are connected with rivers. One interpretation is that the word "Paraguay" comes from the language of the Guaraní Indians who originally inhabited the region, and means "a river that is variously crowned." This is explained by the *camelotes*, or floating islands of water hyacinths, which can be seen on the Paraguay River when it is in flood. Another explanation gives the meaning of Paraguay as simply "the place with the great river."

Rivers form the greater part of Paraguay's borders, but the frontiers have been created largely as a result of the country's devastating wars with its neighbors. Although Paraguay is small, and very dependent on the goodwill of its neighbors, particularly Argentina, to retain its links abroad, this did not prevent the ambitious dictator, Francisco Solano Lopez, from taking on the combined forces of Brazil, Argentina, and Uruguay in the War of the Triple Alliance in 1865. For five years the Paraguayans fought hard. Their courage was legendary; but when defeat came in

14

1870, it was with the loss of three-quarters of the male population of the country, and almost a quarter of its territory.

Equal devastation was brought about in another war in the 1930s. The cause of that war was an area of land called the Chaco, which lies on the border of Paraguay, Bolivia, and Argentina. The Chaco is a wilderness of scrub forest. One writer called it "The Green Hell," a name which has stuck, and hardly anyone, apart from native Indians and one resourceful community of settlers, lives there. However, the Chaco was important to Bolivia, the only other landlocked country in South America, because it could provide a vital link to the sea. By way of the Pilcomayo River and the same river system used by Paraguay, Bolivia could reach the Atlantic Ocean. But the Bolivians needed to own a certain tract of the Chaco to make this possible. In the end there was no real victor in the war, but the Paraguayans, as the stronger side, gained a large area of the Chaco in the final settlement.

The Chaco is a region of almost 100,000 square miles (259,000 square kilometers) of gently undulating plains to the west of the Paraguay River. Today it makes up about two-thirds of Paraguay, but only a small percentage of the population lives there. It is a land of dry grasses and thorny forest growing on sandy soils and clays brought down by the rivers from the Andes Mountains. At times it is scorched brown by the summer sun, and at times it is flooded by the tropical rains. A new highway, the Trans Chaco, has opened up this inhospitable wilderness as it forges a route northwest from Asunción to the Bolivian border. At first it passes

The grasslands and thorny forest of the Chaco.

through the Low Chaco, a flooded forest of palm trees and marshes of water hyacinth. The tall, thin fan palms or carandai grow to an average height of 30 feet (nine meters), though they can be much more, and the hard wood is used in building. There are some *estancias* or large farms in this region where cattle roam and feed among the palms. The largest town in the Chaco is Villa Hayes, capital of the Department Presidente Hayes. Both of these were named after a president of the United States who acted as mediator in the boundary settlement between Argentina and Paraguay after the War of the Triple Alliance.

The Mennonites, a religious group, have settled in the area known as the Middle Chaco. Their main center is the town of Filadelfia, around which are over 100 neatly arranged villages.

16

The settlers are mainly crop farmers, but the natural terrain is scrub forest and cactus. This is the home of Paraguay's most famous tree—the *quebracho*, or axebreaker. It was given this name because the wood is so hard. Here, too, is the bottletree. Its bulbous trunk enables it to conserve enough water to survive long periods of drought. Another native tree is the *palo santo*, or holy tree—so called because its astringent bark and leaves are used as medicines against dysentery and burns.

Beyond the Middle Chaco, to the northwest, is the High Chaco. This is a stunted thorny forest, with an armory of spikes and spines, where there is little shade against the intense summer sun. Heat, drought, and the risk of fire are common hazards. Almost nobody lives there and, despite the highway, there is very little traffic. The whole area has been declared a national park as, largely unexplored and certainly unexploited, it is rich in wildlife.

Fan palms in the Chaco—they can grow to 30 feet (nine meters) and their hard wood is used in building.

The bottletree—its bulbous trunk conserves water, enabling it to survive long periods of drought.

Here, the Chaco lives up to the true meaning of its name—"hunting ground." Roaming in the late afternoon and at night to avoid the heat, and congregating around the water holes are jaguars, pumas, maned wolves, and deer, as well as boars that were first introduced by European settlers and which have become wild. The prehistoric-looking armadillo and the long-nosed anteater are common, as are the otter and the coypu—a rodent that lives in the rivers. And, as in every part of the Chaco, there are countless

18

birds—ibis, herons, toucans, ducks, parrots, parakeets, and many more. Multitudes of insects fill the trees; and on the ground, spiders and snakes hide in the dry, thorny scrub.

It seldom happens that a river can so abruptly divide a country in two as the Paraguay River does. In contrast to the Chaco to the west of the river, the eastern bank is a delightful, fertile garden. When Europeans first discovered this land, they were enchanted by what they described as a natural arcadia—a paradise of green, dense luxuriant forests filled with fruits and a mass of colorful wildlife. Everywhere there was the sound of running water.

The eastern region enjoys a healthy, subtropical climate. Summer temperatures from October to March average between

The *palo santo*, or holy tree—its bark and leaves are used for medicinal purposes.

A maned wolf, one of the many animals that roam wild in the Chaco.

77 and 104 degrees Fahrenheit (25 and 40 degrees Celsius); and winter temperatures range between 50 and 68 degrees Fahrenheit (10 and 20 degrees Celsius). While the Chaco, to the west of the Paraguay River, is subject to alternating periods of drought and flooding, rainfall in the east of the country is plentiful all the year round. It prompted one Paraguayan writer, J. Natalicio Gonzalez, to write that eastern Paraguay is one of the best-watered areas in the world.

This plain in the east between the Paraguay River and the Paraná River makes up the remaining one-third of the republic. A landscape of rounded, forested hills, it lies at an altitude of between 980 and 1,970 feet (300 and 600 meters) on the fringe of

20

the Paraná Plateau which extends over much of southern Brazil. Covered with rich alluvial soil, this is Paraguay's most fertile agricultural zone and it is intensively cultivated.

Most of Paraguay's population of over five million live in this region. Asunción, the capital, is in this zone. So too are the important river towns of Concepción to the north on the Paraguay River, and Encarnación to the southeast on the Paraná River. The only major rail link in the country crosses the plain to connect Asunción to Encarnación, before heading across Argentina to Buenos Aires.

There are thought to be between 40,000 and 60,000 native Indians left in Paraguay. Most of them live in the Chaco, leading a nomadic existence spent in search of a good food supply. When they settle for a short while, they build homes of brushwood and

A street scene in Encarnación, an important town on the Paraná River.

mud, and occasionally they work on the *estancias* or farms. They are friendly and not hostile to travelers or settlers, but mostly they remain hidden from the modern world. In effect their existence, way of life, and attitudes have changed little since their world was first discovered by Europeans over 400 years ago.

2

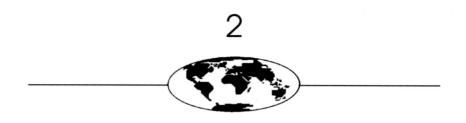

The Jesuit Missions

In 1524 Aleixo Garcia, a Portuguese explorer, with three or four companions, was the first white man to sail up the Paraguay River. He was searching for a route to the Inca Empire in the Andes and, accompanied by a band of some 2,000 Guaraní warriors, he set off across the formidable Chaco. The explorers were lucky and no doubt relieved to find a friendly native people. For their part, the Guaraní, who already had some experience of the Incas, were keen to help the Europeans.

Although a forest people, whose activities were largely farming maize and manioc, hunting game, and fishing, the Guaraní had found time to expand from their original homelands in the eastern plain between the Paraguay and Paraná rivers. They settled to the east, in present-day Brazil, and to the west, where they subdued the hostile native tribes in the Chaco. Spurred on by this success, the Guaraní then ventured into the Andes and made contact with the Incas. For the first time they discovered metal—gold, silver, and copper. These were exactly the valuable treasures which the foreign explorers were seeking. After a successful journey into the Andes, Garcia returned to Paraguay where, for some unexplained reason, he and his companions were killed. But news of the silver spread and it was only a short time before other explorers, notably Sebastian Cabot, also ventured up the Paraguay River. The Spanish emperor, Charles V, then decided to create a settlement from which serious exploration and colonization could be pursued. The first settlement was at present-day Buenos Aires in Argentina, but the Europeans found the surrounding pampas barren and wild, and inhabited by hostile Indians. They moved upstream and, on August 15, 1537, founded a small fort where they could repair their boats.

The fort and town that developed was called Asunción. For about 40 years, it was the headquarters of all the Spanish possessions in southern South America. Today it is the capital of Paraguay. The Spaniards were content. They settled a fertile land, rich with many different fruits and crops, where game and fish were abundant. And they were among friendly people. The Guaraní, too, quickly grew used to the cattle and horses introduced by the Europeans, and they learned some of the crafts of the white man. Soon marriage took place between the two races, and the first *mestizo* children were born. It was a happy union and when, in 1580, Buenos Aires was again settled and later was made the capital of the Spanish provinces, the community at Asunción continued undisturbed.

With less attention and fewer demands from the Spanish crown, the people of the Paraguay province developed their own identity, retaining many of the Indian ways and customs. Paraguay became a separate colony at the beginning of the 17th century, and its governor, Hernando Arias de Saavedra, locally known as Hernandarias, was the first Creole (Spaniard of pure blood born in the colonies) to hold such a position anywhere in Latin America.

It was in this environment that a very remarkable experiment took place. Throughout the New World, members of the Catholic Church accompanied the military in their attempt to colonize the land. The aim of the Church was to convert the natives to Christianity. The first bishop arrived in Asunción in 1556, and he was followed, in 1588, by three Jesuit missionaries. The Jesuits were members of the Roman Catholic Society of Jesus which had been founded by Ignatius Loyola in Rome in 1533. The missionaries set to work among the Guaraní Indians in the upper reaches of the Paraná River, close to the Brazilian frontier, armed only with their faith in God. By 1609, they had persuaded a group of nomadic Guaraní to leave their jungle home and help build the first stone mission. The Indians would live in the mission village where they would be protected from other tribes and from the Portuguese slavers who lived on the other side of the Paraná River in what is now southern Brazil.

The Jesuit strategy was to retain, as far as possible, the Indian tribal system, so when the Indians joined the missions they were organized in chiefdoms. A chief might rule over 20 to 30 families in a mission, totaling about 4,000 people. By the end of the 17th century, there were 30 missions housing approximately 100,000 Indians. The mission villages were built to a pattern. In their sim-

25

A Guaraní Indian girl. The Guaranís's original homelands were in the eastern plain between the Paraguay and Paraná rivers.

plest form the center was dominated by a *plaza* or square where sheep grazed. On one side of the square was the church, usually a towered structure made of stone or hardwood, and on the other three sides were the mud-brick houses in which the Indians lived.

The daily routine included work in the fields, study, prayer, and music. The aim was to create a society in which everyone was treated equally—a form of socialist community. There were individual and communal farms, with everyone taking a turn to farm the "land of God" for the benefit of the church fathers, and the sick and needy. Maize, sugar, fruit, tobacco, and cotton were the main crops, together with the native *yerba maté*, a refreshing tea enjoyed by both Indians and Jesuits, which also became a highly

26

profitable export. In return for their produce, the Indians received food and clothing, and small imported gifts such as knives, scissors, and mirrors.

Some of the Indians were introduced to a classical education, studying in the mission libraries which housed hundreds of books and works of art. Others learned the more practical arts of weaving, boat building, printing, and carpentry. In particular they learned to make musical instruments, as singing and dancing were popular among the Guaraní. From the beginning, the Jesuits recognized and encouraged this. Music could be heard somewhere in the mission village all day long. Even the early morning procession to the fields was a parade of the saints, to the sound of music and chanting.

While music was one form of their artistic expression, the Indians showed even greater skill as craftsmen. Each mission was equipped with a well-supplied workshop, with imported tools (only iron was available locally), and books on art and architecture. The Indians received instruction from Jesuit fathers who were experts in many crafts. Everything was created for the greater glory of God. Magnificent churches were constructed in brick and stone, lined with colorful local paintings. Pulpits and statues were carved in fine native woods or stone, often depicting local forest flora and fauna such as passion flowers, pineapples, palms, and ferns. The sculptured faces of angels, some with distinctly Indian features, hung from painted ceilings and pillars, while beautifully fashioned silver candlesticks and plate ornaments decorated the lavish altars. It has been estimated that some

5,000 images of saints and apostles were kept in the mission churches.

The Jesuits remained in Paraguay for 150 years, until 1767 when King Carlos III of Spain expelled them from the New World. Their very success was their downfall. They had amassed a great deal of power and wealth, and laid themselves open to the criticism that they were a "state within a state." In particular, they formed private armies which they said were for the defense of the missions against the Portuguese slave traders. However, the local Spanish authority could never be sure that the armies would not be used against the crown. The Jesuits were also disliked by members of other religious orders in Paraguay—the Franciscans and Dominicans—who helped to spread rumors of discontent. The Spanish landowners too resented the Jesuits because they controlled the very profitable export trade of the *yerba maté* tea. Not only did the landowners want a share in the trade, but they also coveted the Indian labor force, that worked so well within the missions, for use as slaves. And when Portuguese traders from Brazil attacked missions in order to steal the "slaves," the local Spanish landowners showed their hostility to the Jesuits by doing nothing to help defend the missions.

It was a sad day for the Indians when the Jesuits left. The missions were handed over to civilian administrators and other religious orders, who never treated the Indians as well as the Jesuits had done. One by one the mission villages were raided or burned down, the precious religious artifacts were stolen, the splendid carvings destroyed, and the churches left in ruins. Of the 30 mis-

An 18th-century wooden figure, carved by the Guaraní Indians under instruction from the Jesuits.

sions thriving when the Jesuits left, only eight remained 15 years later. The Indians returned to their forest home, leaving the ruined missions to the mercy of the fast-growing tropical jungle.

And there the story might have ended, but for a program started in the 1970s to restore the Jesuit buildings. Up to the early 1970s, the ruins of Trinidad and nearby Jesús, close to Encarnación, were partly covered by the debris of collapsed masonry and overgrown with subtropical vegetation. Trees grew from one church tower as the roots of vines and climbing plants forced the building blocks apart. Experienced restorers knew it

29

was only a matter of time before the mission would be reduced to rubble. An internationally funded study in 1974 set in motion a program of restoration financed by the Paraguayan government and a West German foundation.

The mission at Trinidad demanded immediate attention. Thought to have been founded around 1706 as a sort of regional capital for the Jesuits, experts believe it was built by the famous Milanese Jesuit architect known in Paraguay as Juan Bautista Primal. As a center, Trinidad was rich and, after the expulsion of the Jesuits, looters moved in. None of the buildings survived their attention. During the restoration, tons of earth were cleared to expose the walls, and it was found that without support many of them needed temporary props. After careful repair and strengthening, the major walls now stand unaided—a tribute to the skill of the original construction. As the restorers cleared away the soil,

Restoration work on the ruins of a Jesuit mission at Trinidad.

they sifted it for treasures and found many stone carvings in pieces. Many of these have been meticulously reassembled and placed in the niches from which they had fallen. One relic, a carved stone pulpit, was found in over 1,500 pieces—now it stands near its original position, and is protected by a permanent shelter. At Jesús, set just a short distance away among rich farmland, the massive church needed less attention. It was to have been the major achievement of the Jesuit builders, but was never finished.

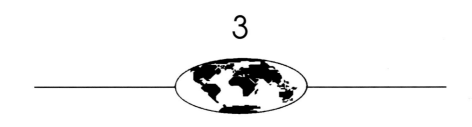

3

Land of Warriors

By the beginning of the 19th century, the Spanish colonies in South America wanted to break away from the Spanish crown and become independent. Many of the other colonies on the continent had greater reason to do this than Paraguay, as their mines and riches had been exploited and their people made to work as slaves. Protected by its location and lack of rich resources, Paraguay had been left largely to its own devices. Even so, there was growing discontent that taxes were still paid to the Spanish crown; and as early as 1721 there had been a revolt followed by 15 years of rebellion in an attempt to overthrow the Spanish governor. The unrest and lack of order allowed the Portuguese in Brazil, always looking for the opportunity to push south across Paraguay's borders, to seize a large area of land in the north, which has remained in Brazil ever since. It was necessary for Paraguay to keep a permanent and expensive defense system, not only against Brazil but also against Argentina. And when, in 1776, Paraguay was made part of the viceroyalty of the Plate

A portrait of Dr. José Gaspar Rodriguez de Francia, the first president of Paraguay, who held power for 26 years.

River, and so found itself under orders from Buenos Aires, this was very deeply resented. Argentina broke away from Spain in 1810, and in 1811 the Argentine General Belgian was sent to subdue the Paraguayans. But he met with fierce and bitter opposition, and retreated to Buenos Aires with his mission unaccomplished. Shortly afterwards, on May 11th, Paraguay made its own decision and independently broke from Spain.

The history of Paraguay from the time of independence until the present day is of a country isolated either by dictatorship or war. The first president, Dr. José Gaspar Rodriguez de Francia, known as *El Supremo*, was an academic who liked to be known as an "algebraist and astronomer." He was an austere man, much feared for the severe punishments meted out to anyone who crossed his path. He ruled with the help of a force of spies, and an army which was at times brutal and ruthless. But he is best remembered as the man who closed the borders of his country to the outside world for the 26 years he held power, until he died in 1840. At a time when the other newly independent republics in South America were opening themselves up to traders from anywhere in the world, Dr. Francia forbade his people all personal and business contact abroad. He feared that foreign influence and liberal ideas would undermine his position. And he may well have been right, for elsewhere in the continent, many of the other countries were torn apart by revolution soon after independence. Indeed, many people now believe that his policy of isolation benefitted Paraguay, as the people learned to be self-sufficient in business and developed a strong sense of national unity.

The next president, Carlos Antonio Lopez, had different ideas, however, and he began to open up Paraguay's frontiers. Even so, a short period of isolation was forced on the country when its neighbor, Argentina, under the fearsome dictator Rosas, closed the Plate River to Paraguayan ships and trade. This stopped when Rosas died in 1852. However, continued hostility from Argentina and Brazil, which were both still anxious to gain more land in Paraguay, influenced Lopez towards building a modern state with a good communications system and transportation network. Foreign scientists and engineers were welcomed to Paraguay. Docks and river forts were established. The first railway, from Asunción to Paraguari, was constructed under the direction of two British engineers and is one of the oldest in the continent. A

Carlos Antonio Lopez, president of Paraguay 1844-1862.

telegraph line was also started. The first Asunción newspaper, *El Paraguayo Independiente*, was printed in 1845. An estimated 400 schools were built and, although most people could still not read or write, Lopez introduced scholarships for the best students to study abroad, especially in scientific subjects. In 1842, while ruling the country as consul, Carlos Antonio Lopez abolished slavery—some 20 years before the United States.

Although he should be credited with laying the foundations of the modern Paraguayan state, Carlos Antonio Lopez was rather less successful in conducting foreign affairs. He was mistrustful of his neighbors and, partly because he had grown up during the

35

time of Dr. Francia's isolationist policy, Lopez had little international experience before taking power. In 1855 he was threatened by a major Brazilian naval expedition on the Paraná River. Then, in 1858, a U.S. flotilla was sent to support an American citizen in conflict with the president over the export of *yerba maté* tea. Rightly, Lopez felt that the monopoly in this profitable business should be in the hands of the Paraguayans, not foreigners. In 1859 Lopez also came into conflict with the British when he imprisoned a naval captain in Asunción, accusing him of conspiracy against the president. The British were angered by this move and, in retaliation, the consul in Buenos Aires decided to teach Lopez a lesson. He took the president's eldest son hostage, Francisco Solano Lopez, who happened to be visiting Argentina.

As a child, Francisco Solano Lopez, the eldest of Carlos Antonio's four children, was pampered, spoiled, and undisciplined. He was frequently in trouble, particularly with girls, and his father always bailed him out. His "punishment" was often to be sent on some mission or other to keep him out of trouble. He had, however, grown to be a capable soldier (he was a general at the age of 18, and general-in-chief of the Paraguayan army and Minister of War at 26), with some talent for diplomacy and languages. On this occasion he had just succeeded in bringing to an end an internal conflict between two Argentinian generals. As a result he had been feted by his grateful neighbors and had set out as a hero on his journey back to Paraguay in a steamer he had just bought called the *Tacuari*. The ship, with the president's son on board, was kidnapped in an audacious move by the British consul. To get his "hostage" son back, Carlos Antonio Lopez had to agree to some humiliating terms imposed by the British.

It was already evident that Francisco Solano Lopez was being trained by the family as a successor to his father. As part of his preparation for the job, Francisco Solano was sent in 1853 as an ambassador at large to Europe. His mission was to put Paraguay on the international map and to bring back the equipment and machinery necessary to make Paraguay a modern state.

In these duties he succeeded quite well, but his journey to

Francisco Solano Lopez, president of Paraguay 1862-1870, who led his country into the disastrous War of the Triple Alliance.

Europe had a profound and lasting effect on him for other reasons. First he was received by the French emperor Napoleon III, nephew of Napoleon Bonaparte who was his boyhood idol, and on whom he shaped his ambitions for the future. Second, he met an Irish lady, Eliza Lynch, who became his mistress for life and bore him four children. Eliza, a lady of good background who experienced considerable hardship during the potato famine in Ireland, had made her own way into the aristocratic circles of Britain and France, and sought greater adventure. She eagerly set sail to join Francisco Solano Lopez in the tiny, unknown South American republic. But whereas Francisco Solano was greeted everywhere with fanfare and ceremony, his mistress encountered the cold hostility of the Lopez family. She was, after all, already married to someone else and the family wanted Francisco Solano to take a Paraguayan girl as his wife. For Eliza Lynch the first few years in Paraguay were lonely and desolate. She only received a degree of respect with the death of Carlos Antonio Lopez in 1862, when Francisco Solano Lopez seized power and made himself the next president.

Paraguay now had an ambitious and popular young president who was a good soldier and a capable diplomat with international connections. It seemed that the country could look forward to years of prosperity and progress. Unhappily, however, always lurking in the background was the unresolved international border problem that existed in the region of the Plate River between Argentina, Uruguay, and Paraguay, between Paraguay and Brazil in the east, and Paraguay and Bolivia in the west. The frontiers between these countries had never been properly defined at the time of independence, and were open to abuse. Dr. Francia had ignored the problem by shutting the country off and so not exposing it to any confrontation. Carlos Antonio Lopez, unwilling to commit his country to outright war, had used his political skills to sidestep the real issues. But Francisco Solano Lopez, ambitious, not so astute and supported in every way by a determined Eliza, saw himself as the future Napoleon of South America.

Even as Carlos Antonio was dying, he tried to warn his son. His last words to Francisco Solano advised against war. "There are many problems waiting to be aired," he said. "Do not try to solve them by the sword but by the pen, chiefly with Brazil." By ignoring this advice, Francisco Solano Lopez led his country into the disastrous War of the Triple Alliance. The war was triggered when Marshal Lopez, as Francisco Solano now called himself, decided to go to the aid of Uruguay. Like Paraguay, Uruguay is a tiny country bordered by the powerful republics of Argentina and Brazil. From the time of its independence in 1828, Uruguay had been subjected to constant attacks by each of its neighbors in turn. When, in 1864, Brazil again sent an armed force into Uruguay, Marshal Lopez decided to seize a Brazilian ship on the Paraguay River. He also dispatched his army across Argentine territory to invade southern Brazil. To offend Argentina in this way was a fatal mistake. Brazil, Uruguay, and Argentina joined forces against Paraguay and war was declared.

From the beginning, the odds against Marshal Lopez were overwhelming. But he was fighting on home ground and he was the

The country home of Eliza Lynch, Francisco Solono Lopez's mistress. This building is now the Gran Hotel del Paraguay in Asunción.

head of a nation of warriors—the Guaraní had always been coura-geous and fierce in battle. He was a ruthless leader, demanding absolute loyalty and determination from his own men. He carried out terrifying acts of cruelty, never accepting defeat and executing any of his men who survived a lost battle. He sent his troops on suicide missions, and in May 1866 he lost almost 20,000 of his best men in one battle. Cholera epidemics and starvation added to the huge losses. Women were called in to work in the fields, to make clothes, and sometimes to fight. Eliza Lynch, who followed the Marshal throughout the war, is said to have created her own army of women. With the increasing inevitability of defeat, the Marshal became even more ruthless—perhaps even a little mad. He feared conspiracies and executed many of his followers,

40

including his own family—mother and brothers. Eliza remained loyal to the end and when the Marshal was killed in action, in 1870 at Cerro Cora in northern Paraguay, she was there to bury him, scraping out a shallow grave with her own hands.

Paraguay was thus ravaged and devastated. Of an original population of approximately 500,000, less than half had survived. There were only about 30,000 men left in the country. And in the peace treaty that followed the war Paraguay lost territory to both Brazil and Argentina. For eight years Paraguay remained occupied by its neighbors, and for the moment the frontier disputes were put aside.

In the few peaceful years that followed, there was time to consider alternative ways of governing the country, and two political parties evolved. This period has been described as the golden era of Paraguayan literature. Notable intellectuals like Cecilio Báez and Eusebio Ayala—both of whom became presidents of the republic—used their writing skills to spread the political word. In 1874, a war hero named General Bernardino Caballero founded the first party—the conservative *Colorados* or "Reds"—from people who associated themselves with the heroic efforts of Marshal Lopez to defend the country. The other party, the *Liberales* or "Blues," was founded by Cecilio Báez in 1887. The *Liberales* dominated the political scene for almost 30 years, from 1904 until 1932, when the Chaco War broke out.

Bolivia, the other landlocked country in South America, desperately needed an outlet to the sea. In the War of the Pacific some 50 years earlier, it had lost its Pacific port and coastline to

Chile. The only other way Bolivia could reach the sea was by the Plate River system to the Atlantic Ocean. The Chaco region, which could provide the essential link in the route, was therefore important to the Bolivians, whose determination to get it increased when it was suggested that oil deposits existed there. Naturally, the Paraguayans did not want to lose the Chaco, and they also wanted to restore military morale following their defeat in the War of the Triple Alliance. Each side staked its claim and war ensued.

The war lasted for three years but neither side had the satisfaction of total victory. The Paraguayans almost won, partly because of the same tenacity and courage of the Guaraní warriors, partly because of the leadership and inventiveness of the Paraguayan Colonel José Felix Estigarribia. But the Paraguayans could not

A British-built tank used in the Chaco War (1932-35), now displayed in Asunción as a permanent reminder of the devastation caused.

conquer the mountain homelands of the Bolivians, and so an armistice was agreed. According to the peace treaty, Paraguay kept at least three-quarters of the Chaco, but the cost in lives and casualties had again been very heavy.

4

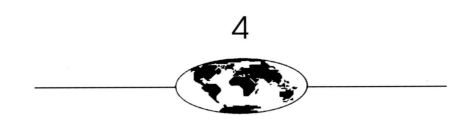

Paraguay under President Stroessner

For almost 20 years, from the end of the Chaco War, the political scene in Paraguay was chaotic. Despite having led the country to victory, the Liberals were ousted immediately afterwards. They were guilty of paying too much attention to war heroes, and not enough to the peasants in the front line. The poor of the country, who had given their best, now demanded social reforms such as education and medical care, but the Liberals would not listen. The Liberal president, Eusebio Ayala, was deposed in a coup and his place taken by Colonel Franco who was a popular war hero. Because the coup occurred in the month of February, Franco's followers became known as *Febristas*, and their name is associated with the idea of the "New Paraguay." The policies of the "New Paraguay" included land reform. A start was made in breaking up the large estates and giving the peasants their own small plots of land. Also, a decree was passed to recognize trade unions and give their members the "right to strike." The Paraguayan

Workers' Confederation (CPT) was subsequently formed. Franco and the *Febristas* were not long in power, but every leader from then on had to take account of the social movement they had begun.

The Liberals returned to power in 1939, led by the war hero Marshal Estigarribia. Estigarribia was an astute politician and well aware of the value of the social reform program. His plans were similar to those of the *Febristas*, but on a larger scale. His aim was that every Paraguayan family should own a plot of land. He wanted to open up the country, extend its transportation system, create a merchant marine, and develop the oilfields in the Chaco. Faced with members of his own party who disagreed with such reforms, he temporarily made himself dictator and, in 1940, introduced a new constitution. Just two months later, he was killed in a plane crash. Had he lived, perhaps he could have saved Paraguay from the next 16 turbulent years.

From 1940 to 1948, General Morinigo was president of Paraguay. At first he was appointed only as "temporary president." Although he had no planned strategy, he was an opportunist—a man who survived by political wheeling and dealing, manipulating competitors, enemies, and their supporters. It does, however, seem that he was the right man for the job at the time. The Second World War had broken out in 1939, and the countries of South America were divided between those who supported the Allies and those who supported the Axis powers. Argentina was known to support the Germans; and Paraguay, so close to Argentina in many ways, soon found that many countries were anxious to enlist its support. Brazil, Argentina's oldest rival, offered loans for public works. More importantly, Paraguay's friendship and cooperation was cultivated by the United States. It was vital for the United States to have a strategic base near Argentina. Money and technical assistance began to flow into Paraguay, to help the building of roads and ports, and to develop agriculture and the health services. Morinigo's opportunist talents were well deployed. On the one hand, he gratefully accepted these approaches and finally declared himself for the Allies. But, on the other hand, he remained on good terms with Argentina throughout the war. This was essential for the Paraguayans who can never allow themselves to forget how dependent they are on Argentina and the Plate River for their access to the sea.

Although a good percentage of the foreign loans and gifts were diverted away from the medical and agricultural programs for which they were intended (Morinigo secured his own position by using the funds for the armed forces), Paraguay became more prosperous because of the war. In particular, there was an increased demand from America and Europe for exports of hides, hard woods, cotton, and tinned meat, and many small businessmen benefitted from this upsurge in trade.

When the Second World War ended in 1945, it was predictable that chaos would again erupt in Paraguay. Morinigo had managed to keep himself in power, but only by using brutal dictatorial measures. He had exiled many of his opponents, and his enemies ranged from the Liberals and *Febristas*, to the trade unions and the press. For once, these groups put aside their differences and

Alfredo Stroessner (*center*), president of Paraguay 1954-1989.

joined together for the express purpose of getting rid of the president. They led an unsuccessful revolt in 1947, sometimes described as a civil war, which left thousands dead. Morinigo was finally deposed by his own party, the *Colorados* in 1948. In the next six years, Paraguay had six presidents and the turmoil only ended when the commander-in-chief of the armed forces, General Alfredo Stroessner, became president in 1954.

Having come to power against this background of intrigue, bitter in-party fighting, coup, and counter-coup, it is remarkable that President Stroessner remained in control for over 30 years.

Alfredo Stroessner, the son of a German immigrant who arrived

47

in Paraguay in the 1890s, fought in the Chaco War earning medals and commendations. Recognized as a good leader and organizer, he remained in the military after the war. He became Major Stroessner in 1940.

Major Stroessner had a great capacity for work and was noted for his unusual physical strength and his "spirit of initiative." Unlike some of his colleagues about this time, he never sought the limelight, preferring to remain discreetly in the background until the time was right. His diligence was rewarded with the right promotions and, by the age of 33, he was commander of Paraguay's chief artillery unit. And so, when Morinigo was faced with revolt and civil war in 1947, Major Stroessner was in a key position to defeat the rebels and earn the president's praise. About this time, he allied himself with the Colorado Party and became more openly involved in politics. In 1951, the Colorado president, Federico Chaves, appointed him commander-in-chief of the armed forces, and his name began to be a feature on the international scene, with visits to Uruguay, Brazil, Argentina, and the United States.

It was one thing to become president of Paraguay at the age of 41 in August 1954, but it was another to stay president for any length of time. In the beginning, President Stroessner secured his position by ruling with a firm hand. Like his predecessors he exiled many of his political and military opponents, and used the army to put down revolts encouraged by these exiled groups. He introduced a state of siege that lasted for his entire term, and any form of opposition, such as the press or student protests was harshly suppressed. On the one occasion that a general strike

48

The Government Palace in Ascunción.

was threatened, Stroessner's police force arrested hundreds of workers.

Officially, the president of Paraguay is elected every five years. During President Stroessner's rule, the constitution was changed to make him continually eligible for reelection. His reelection was then little more than a formality. Even so, at election time he made a point of canvassing the people for support, as it is compulsory for everyone over the age of 18 to vote.

President Stroessner had wide-ranging powers. As one observer said: "Every military assignment and promotion, every party meeting, resolution or election, every majority member of Congress, every legislative act, every judgeship, every executive post, and every cabinet decision must bear his seal of approval." To assist him in running the affairs of state, Stroessner appointed a council of state, made up of nine members, to act as his advisers.

Political parties were allowed to exist but the activities of opposition groups like the *Febristas* and Liberals were restricted. This meant that elections resulted inevitably in a victory for the Colorado Party of President Stroessner, who took up the majority of seats in Congress. The opposition parties took the few remaining seats. Opposition to President Stroessner's rule was voiced mostly by the Roman Catholic Church or the students. The press was censored.

President Stroessner's presence was felt everywhere in Paraguay. His name was given to towns, bridges, buildings, a river steamer, and the international airport. His portrait hung in most offices and many private homes. And above the office buildings in Asunción there was a neon-lit sign that declared *Paz, Trabajoy, Bienestar con Stroessner* ("Peace, Work, and Welfare with Stroessner"). While recognizing that there were disadvantages in the system, many Paraguayans agreed with the slogan and were grateful for an orderly and stable society. Some, of course, did not.

Over the last 45 years, many advances were made in Paraguay. When President Stroessner came to power, the country was in a state of economic chaos and one of his first acts was to reform the nation's finances. With help from international banks and by imposing a rigorous domestic program involving cuts in public spending and increased taxation, the Paraguayan currency—the *guarani*—became one of the most stable in South America. This was essential if Paraguay was to develop a transportation system that would open up the country and help expand the economy, and introduce the social reforms that were necessary to modernize the state.

A very top priority was the need to lessen Paraguay's dependence on Argentina for access to the sea. Consequently Stroessner agreed with the Brazilians to the building of the "Friendship Bridge" over the Paraná River. In this way, Asunción has a road connection with Sao Paulo in Brazil and with ports such as Paranaguá on Brazil's Atlantic coast. At the same time, plans were developed for the Trans Chaco Highway running north from Asunción through the largely unexplored Chaco wilderness to Bolivia. Small roads were constructed to link up the towns in the interior of the country and, between 1955 and 1975, the road network was expanded from 725 to 4,646 miles (1,166 to 7,477 kilometers), with the paved proportion increasing tenfold.

To demonstrate how backward the country was and how much has been improved in the last 45 years, one need look no further than Asunción, the capital. In 1958, fresh water was being brought into the town in jugs and cans carried in carts or tied to the back of donkeys. Now the city boasts fresh, piped running water and storm drains. There has also been a serious attempt to improve medical facilities in rural areas, and today many villages have access to clinics.

Throughout the country, President Stroessner personally opened many new schools, and education reached some of the more remote parts of the country. Education is free and compulsory but as teachers and equipment are in short supply, many people are still unable to read or write. An added problem is that lessons are taught in Spanish, although many Paraguayans speak Guaraní as their first language. In addition, a great deal still has to be done to improve housing, as many families live in poor conditions with neither electricity nor running water.

In 1988 dissension within the Colorado Party divided the traditional members from the more militant in the party. The traditional members wanted a more accessible and tolerant form of government. The militant group supported the continuation of Stroessner's policies. The traditionalists eventually broke away from the party and gathered enough support to overthrow Stroessner in a coup on February 3, 1989.

One of the military generals, Andrés Rodriguez led the coup and became president in the elections. Stroessner went into exile. Rodriguez drafted a new constitution in 1992 which included democratic policies. He declared freedom of the press, legalized all political parties, repealed repressive laws, and freed political prisoners.

In 1993 the first free multiparty elections in Paraguay's history were held. Juan Carlos Wasmosy of the Colorado Party was elected president. Controversy over the Colorado Party's links with the military ended in 1995 when legislation was passed banning the military from joining political parties or participating in politics.

The transition to democracy has not been easy for Paraguay

with constant attempts by the military to regain control. Because Wasmosy's Colorado Party did not have a majority in the Congress there have been many legislative stalemates. Unions have gone on general strikes to protest low wages and high inflation. The people of Paraguay are ready to benefit from their new-found democracy.

5

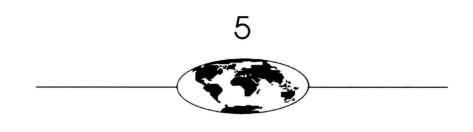

The Paraguayans

The population of Paraguay is small—just over five million people. (Compare this with a country like Japan, which is slightly smaller than Paraguay and has a population of 125 million.) The devastation of the War of the Triple Alliance and the Chaco War left the country with only a fraction of its male population, and the male-female ratio is only now returning to normal. In addition many Paraguayans have left the country in the last 40 years (some estimates suggest as many as 25 percent of all Paraguayans live overseas) either as political exiles or for economic reasons. Many have gone to Brazil and Argentina—countries which have developed industrially and commercially and are in a position to offer work with better pay than Paraguay.

Paraguay has never experienced the same full-scale waves of immigrants from Europe as other countries in South America. This is partly because it lacks the resources that tempt people to settle and colonize, and partly because of its "closed borders" policy and the wars that dominated the country in the 19th century.

Nevertheless, after the War of the Triple Alliance, there were attempts to attract agricultural workers to Paraguay.

In one scheme, English contractors were offered five dollars per head for recruiting farmers from the Lincolnshire area in England. But instead of venturing to Lincolnshire, the unscrupulous traders collected 800 people from the East End of London and shipped them off to Asunción. As city people, the Londoners stood little chance of coping in the Paraguayan countryside without food or shelter. Some eventually made their way to Buenos Aires helped by British families living there who learned of their plight. Many died from illness, and of the original 800 men, women, and children, only two families remained in Paraguay. Another scheme brought colonists from Australia who contributed all their personal possessions to fund the creation of a socialist-style community in Paraguay. The scheme met with some success. Houses were built and fields cultivated. But soon people became discontented with the "New Australia." The rules of the community were rigid; and life, particularly for the women, was lonely and hard. People drifted away, some settling elsewhere in Paraguay, others returning to Australia.

During the 20th century, immigrants have arrived in Paraguay from distant countries such as Korea and Japan, but the most successful attempt at colonization in Paraguay has been by the Mennonite community. The Mennonites are members of a religious sect which originated in Switzerland. Their customs are similar to those of the Quakers. In the 1920s, when they were looking

for somewhere to settle where they could practice their religion without interference, the Paraguayan authorities offered them a tract of land of over 300,000 acres (120,000 hectares) in the Chaco. The scrub forest was difficult land to develop but the Paraguayans offered the Mennonites generous tax advantages and immigration facilities. They could develop the land as they

56

wished and could live, in a sense, as a "country within a country." The community has its own rules and philosophy, within which military service is forbidden.

The Mennonites worked hard. They also suffered considerably. Because they do not believe in using force, they could not defend themselves against the local, and often hostile, Indians. The Chaco foxes were often a problem too, scavenging and seeking shelter. But the sect survived and prospered. They built houses which were solid and long-lasting, cleared and cultivated the land, and raised cattle. Today around 11,000 Mennonites, together with as many native Paraguayans, live in and around the town of Filadelfia, about 250 miles (400 kilometers) northwest of Asunción. The road to Filadelfia is paved all the way, and around the town neatly painted one-story buildings stand in cultivated green fields. The Mennonites have established an efficient farming cooperative and grow crops such as cotton, sorghum, and castor beans that can survive long periods of drought. They have a small dairy industry, and any surplus dairy products such as cheese and butter are sent to Asunción. The community also has its own banks, schools, and hospitals, and the people speak to each other in a rural German dialect.

The population of the Chaco is made up mainly of the Mennonites and their Indian neighbors, and only a tiny percentage of Paraguay's total population lives there. It is difficult to estimate the number of Indians who may now be left in Paraguay. There are still small communities in eastern Paraguay and the total is probably between 40,000 and 60,000. However, it is certain that this number is decreasing as the land is opened up. Groups like the Guayaki, Ayoreo, and Chamococo are in danger of disappearing. Some tribes like the Ache are settled on reservations, while others like the Toba-Maskoy of the central Chaco have been in dispute with the government over the land on which they live. It has always been difficult to resolve the question of who owns the land on which Indians live. For many years the Indians have moved from one place to another, in search of work and a place to grow a few crops. A first step has been taken towards settling these disputes, however, with a law stating that Indians can own land. Inevitably the Indians's way of life is affected by their contact with western society and slowly a process of integration is taking place.

Integration has never been a problem between the Guaraní Indians and the Spanish conquerors. From the beginning, the two races mixed easily, married and, in producing the first *mestizos*, created the first Paraguayans. The Guaraní were friendly, outgoing, and energetic. The Spaniards were pleased to settle in a beautiful land and readily accepted into their culture the legends of the Guaraní people. The relationship has remained harmonious and the people of Paraguay today are unique in South America. The Indian culture has remained strong and the Guaraní element features in many ways.

Perhaps the most obvious symbol of this cultural mix is that Paraguay has two dominant languages, Spanish and Guaraní, and almost everyone is bilingual. Spanish is the official language and

58

A *mestizo* girl—part Spanish, part Guaraní Indian. The two races have mixed easily in Paraguay, with the result that there are none of the racial tensions found in many other countries.

Guaraní is the language used in the home, and predominantly in rural areas. Spanish is the formal language, Guaraní the language that expresses emotion. So much of the best Paraguayan literature is written in Guaraní, and there is a Guaraní theater. Guaraní is the language of the soccer field or, as one poet wrote, "The Paraguayans love, hate, and fight in Guaraní." The Paraguayan unit of currency is also called the *guaraní*; and the Hotel Guaraní in Asunción was one of the first modern high-rise buildings in the country.

A long-standing tradition in Paraguay is the sociable custom of drinking *yerba maté* tea. Yerba maté comes from the leaves of the

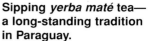

Sipping *yerba maté* tea—a long-standing tradition in Paraguay.

yerba tree, a relative of the European holly which, since the time of the Spaniards, has been important as a profitable export. But the legends of the yerba were known to the Guaraní long before the Spaniards arrived. One is the story of Caá Yara, a beautiful young girl whose parents took her to live in seclusion in the forest, thus protecting her from the evils of the world. There she was found by a Guaraní god who, disguised as a traveler, was treated with great kindness by the girl's parents. In order to repay them, and learning of their concern for their daughter, he made Caá Yara immortal and her spirit entered the yerba tree—known as caá in Guaraní.

60

Yerba leaves are hand-picked (to ensure that only those of the finest quality are selected) and then dried on wooden racks above a simple outdoor oven. The dried yerba is then milled to a fine powder ready for sale in the shops and markets. Yerba can be mixed with either hot or cold water and makes a pale green, distinctly bitter infusion. It may be drunk from cups or glasses, though the Paraguayans most commonly use vessels made of cow horn or a vegetable gourd which are also called *matés*. Sometimes the *matés* are decorated with silverwork and may have a loop so

A Paraguayan farmer inspecting his *yerba* trees.

they can be hooked to a belt. These days, however, they are usually simple in style.

Yerba maté tea is made by half filling the vessel with powdered yerba and adding water. The mixture is stirred with a drinking tube, or *bombilla*, which is complete with a built-in filter. A good suck on the bombilla is all that is needed to get a refreshing drink. Drinking *maté* and passing both the *bombilla* and the *maté* around a group of friends is a ritual that takes place many times a day, in town and country. Visitors are always invited to join in.

Another Guaraní legend is connected with the making of Nanduti lace for which Paraguay is famous. In many villages outside Asunción–particularly at Itauguá–ladies can be seen in the doorways, in their rocking chairs, working on the frames from which they produce a delicate handmade lace. According to the legend, a Paraguayan girl's lover failed to appear on their wedding day. She searched for him in the forests and, finding his body at nightfall, stayed with him until daybreak. As the sun rose she saw that his body was covered by a glistening coverlet of spider webs, which she determined to copy with a needle and thread. And so she made the first Nanduti lace as a shroud.

The legend helps explain the word *nanduti* which in Guaraní means "spider's web." But it was the Spaniards who brought lace-making to Paraguay. And the designs used today reflect ancient traditions of country life. "Ostrich plumage," "foot prints of oxen," and "grains of rice" are some of the motifs woven by the Paraguayan women. Another craft is *Aho-poi*, a cotton homespun

62

Making Nanduti lace. Although lacemaking was introduced into Paraguay by the Spaniards, Nanduti lace is associated with an old Guaraní legend.

cloth, often hand embroidered in a variety of colors. It is used to make blouses and shirts, tablecloths, and other household linen.

Paraguayans love to play music. Their favorite instruments are the harp and guitar introduced to the country by the Spaniards. In the cool of the evening, from the corner of a colonial-style courtyard, it is not at all unusual to hear the melodious rhythm of the native polka dances, and the *Guaraní* folklore songs. For traditional dances, such as the "bottle dance," the women dress in

63

bright, full skirts with flowers in their hair and masses of beads. For this particular dance, bottles attached to each other are piled on top of the dancer's head. With skillful balance, she sways gently in time with the music.

Paraguayans also enjoy their festivals, which are held at important times in the Roman Catholic calendar and on May 14 to celebrate independence. A feature of the religious celebrations are colorful processions in which the statue of the patron saint of the village or town is carried around the streets, bedecked with colored streamers and flowers.

Although there is much traditional culture in Paraguay, the people also participate in many modern sports. Probably the most

Paraguayans in colorful fiesta dress.

A comic bullfight, part of a fiesta held in Asunción. Bullfights (comic or otherwise) are a popular entertainment in Paraguay.

popular, as in every part of South America, is soccer. This is played by children on any spare patch of land as well as by the professional teams in the main stadium in Asunción. Bullfights and rodeos always draw a good crowd, and Paraguayans are good horsemen. There are also many water sports to choose from in "the place with the great river," even in the heart of Asunción.

6

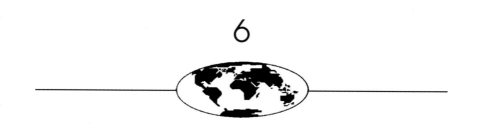

Asunción

Asunción, Paraguay's tiny capital, lies on the east bank of the Paraguay River, not far from the point on the opposite bank where the Pilcomayo flows in from the Chaco. By chance Asunción is placed in the center of South America, halfway between the Caribbean Sea and Tierra del Fuego, and at an equal distance from both the Pacific and Atlantic Oceans.

The city is built on seven low hills, rising behind a large natural lagoon called the Bay of Asunción. While the lower levels of the capital, including riverside homes and some local soccer pitches, remain subject to flooding, the bay provides an excellent harbor away from the strong current of the river. The site was chosen by the Spanish explorer Juan Salazar in 1537 and the city, founded on August 15 of the same year, was named Nuestra Senora Santa Maria de la Asunción (Our Lady Saint Mary of the Ascension).

Many of the capital's important buildings stand on the high ground overlooking the bay. Parks filled with flowering trees, particularly the mauve jacaranda and pink-blossoming *lapacho* tree, provide a relaxed and informal tropical background. The grey-painted Government Palace is set back from the traffic behind lawns and ornamental shrubs. The red, white, and blue national flag, unique in that it carries a different emblem on either side, flies proudly at the top of a central tower furnished with pinnacles. There is no surrounding fence or wire and Paraguayans and visitors alike are permitted to walk as far as the simply decorated entrance hall. Known locally as the Palacio Lopez, after the former president Francisco Solano Lopez who ordered its construction, the building is the work of a British architect, Alonso Taylor, and was begun in 1860, at a time when Britain was deeply involved with commerce and construction in South America. Construction was held up by the War of the Triple Alliance, and the building was eventually completed in 1892. The president's office is in the Government Palace and state receptions are held there.

Not far from the Government Palace is another grand building, the Legislative Palace. Situated in the Plaza Constitucion, this occupies a fine position facing the bay. It is the center of government and stands on the site of the historic *Cabildo* or council chamber of the 16th century.

Behind the Avenida Costanera, as this river-edged recreation and historic zone is called, other streets and squares of Asunción are laid out in a grid fashion. Palma Street is always crowded as it is the center of the exchange houses, where it is possible to deal in all the world's major currencies. The latest rates of exchange,

The Legislative Palace, overlooking the Bay of Asunción.

which can vary rapidly in South America, are flashed on television monitor screens facing the crowds. This is the traditional center of the city, with the Plaza de los Heroes (Square of the Heroes) acting like a magnet to traffic, sightseers, and the busy *Asunceros* (people of Asunción) alike. In one corner, the Pantheon of the Heroes, a building based on Les Invalides in Paris and containing the tombs of various presidents including Carlos Antonio Lopez and his son Francisco, is guarded by two immaculately uniformed soldiers. A perpetual flame of remembrance beside the door honors the dead leaders and the Paraguayan soldiers killed in the War of the Triple Alliance and the War of the Chaco. On certain weekends, Palma Street is closed to traffic and Asunceros come to town

68

in the thousands. Vendors of every kind of trinket and handicraft line the pavement. Women bearing piles of fruit in baskets balanced on their heads step nimbly through the crowd, while local pop-music groups, covered by television cameras, test their latest tunes on the students. Street collections for charities, common in Europe but a rarity in South America, are accepted readily in Asunción and on these holidays find many supporters.

Of the earlier history, few relics have survived, though in a side street within a few paces of the crowded Palma Street is the whitewashed, single-story, tiled house in which the struggle for inde-

The Plaza de los Héroes, with the magnificent Pantheon building—the traditional center of Asunción.

pendence was plotted. Now a museum, the *Casa de la Independencia* (House of Independence) contains important relics of the colonial period, as well as curiosities including the wheels of the carriage used by Eliza Lynch. Madame Lynch, as she is usually remembered, had a country home which is now part of the Gran Hotel del Paraguay in a residential suburb. Two large, elegantly decorated rooms, which are said to have been Madame Lynch's private theater, have survived.

While in every sense Asunción has all the symbols of a capital, including the government buildings and central offices of industry and banking, in many respects it remains unchanged and outside the mainstream of world affairs. New buildings, many of them skyscrapers of 15 or more floors and constructed as the result of a recent economic boom, have transformed the skyline. New

The interior of the *Casa de la Independencia*, Asunción, the house in which the struggle for Paraguayan independence was plotted.

The wheels of Eliza Lynch's carriage—one of the curiosities of the *Casa de la Independencia*.

houses, and a growing middle class have come within the past 20 years. So Asunción is spreading far outside the early riverside city limits. Yet slums, the greatest blight of most South American capitals, have not yet had the opportunity to grow. With the recent changes in the country's fortunes, the major trunk routes leading from the city are being improved, so that the outlying villages and suburbs, once very rural, are now being absorbed into the metropolitan area.

It is often said that it is the people, not the buildings, that make a city. The Guaraní heritage of the Asunceros sets them apart from any other South American city dwellers and this, combined

71

with a broad European background, makes it difficult to pinpoint the origins of many Paraguayans. The most immediately outstanding of all are the few true indigenous Indians of the Maca tribe who live on an island reservation, and come into the city to trade their colorful handicrafts. The Maca are best recognized by their Indian features, long hair, and relatively simple dress. Back in their village the Indians are something of a tourist attraction and visitors must pay to come to their island. The Maca women wear only a skirt while the men wear colored shirts and shorts, which is their nearest equivalent to 20th-century respectability.

Asunción is often regarded as a backwater in the sphere of the arts, education, and entertainment. At one time it seemed that all Paraguayans were exporting their talents. Musicians such as the

The skyline of modern Asunción, transformed by skyscrapers.

A Maca Indian woman.

trio Los Paraguayos traveled widely in the 1950s, making the traditional harp and guitar music famous worldwide. However, such music is close to the hearts of the Asunceros and Asunción boasts many restaurants, open-air bars, and cafés where the music is played. In addition, both the National and Catholic Universities are located in Asunción, as are most of the cultural institutions such as the Conservatory of Music and the National Academy of Fine Arts.

Because of its position on the Paraguay River, Asunción has always enjoyed good communications with boat services as far north as Corumba on the edge of Brazil's Mato Grosso, and downstream to Buenos Aires. In addition, a bridge now crosses

73

Asunción's splendid railway station, built in the early 1860s at the instigation of President Francisco Solano Lopez.

the Paraguay River 10 miles (17 kilometers) above Asunción, linking up with the Trans Chaco Highway on the other side of the river.

The international airport, Silvio Pettirossi, services flights to most South American capitals, Europe, and the United States. In contrast to the soaring concrete buttresses of the airport, Asunción boasts a unique railway station built at the instigation of Francisco Solano Lopez in the early 1860s. The main line runs 231 miles (370 kilometers) to Encarnación, although it was not completed until 1911 because of financial setbacks and delays caused by the War of the Triple Alliance. Since 1914, with the creation of a railway ferry service across the Paraná, the line has linked Asunción to Buenos Aires—a total distance of 906 miles

74

(1,450 kilometers). Around the railway station in Asunción, time seems to have passed by with few changes. At 12:15 precisely on weekdays, a steam train clatters smartly from beneath the ornate portico and down the middle of a street. Cars, pedestrians, and horse-drawn carts get only a whistle blast warning before the puffing steam giant, complete with showers of sparks, thunders by. The locomotives are British-made, some dating from as late as 1953, and designed to burn wood. Paraguay has plenty of wood from the forests and the locomotives will become redundant only when the line has been electrified. Until then the trains, including the "long distance" to Encarnación and the "international" to

A wood-burning steam train clattering out of Asunción station.

Buenos Aires, will continue to be among the last in the world which still remain steam-hauled.

The population of Asunción is now approaching one million, and the demand for services is increasing. Fresh food grown in the surrounding rich agricultural land is brought daily to markets in the city from several small attractive towns. The roads take an ever-increasing burden of heavy traffic, though fortunately such towns as Itauguá, famous for its Nanduti lace, remain unspoiled as the highway keeps away from the center. Similarly, Caacupé with its grand basilica housing an image of the Madonna said to

A market in Caacupé where religious articles are sold. The basilica housing the blue madonna can be seen in the background.

A typical yellow vintage tramcar. Despite their age, these are still a popular means of transportation in Asunción.

have miraculous powers, is still peaceful as the thousands of pilgrims who visit the shrine can attest. But, with the electrification of the villages and the weekend influx of relatively prosperous city dwellers, changes in rural Paraguay cannot be far away—particularly in the area close to Asunción. Already, villages like San Bernardino on the shores of Lake Ypacara, only 30 minutes from the center of Asunción, have been developed with clubs, weekend homes, and boating facilities.

This may seem a long way from the bloody days of the war hero Francisco Solano Lopez and Eliza Lynch, but in Asunción tradition and progress often appear side by side, if not hand in hand. Beneath the mirror silvered windows of some faceless international giant, vintage trolleys rumble along decrepit rails. Sparks may flash from bad contacts, but the yellow-painted, near-museum pieces are favored by the downtown traveler. And in this city of unabashed contrasts, it is still possible to stop at a street corner to buy a *maté* of crushed medicinal plants from a lady whose Guaraní ancestry means she prefers to speak Guaraní rather than Spanish.

7

A Farming Community

Paraguay's economy is essentially based on agriculture and, outside Asunción, most people work as small farmers. Most of the population live in the east on the plain that lies between the Paraguay and Paraná rivers. Intensive farming takes place only in a small area close to Asunción; although in the southern region, around Encarnación, the communities of largely European origin have developed fine and productive land. In total, only 6 percent of the country is cultivated arable land. Pasture covers approximately a quarter of the land and the rest is forest. Statistics in the early 1980s show that large estates covering some 66.6 million acres (27 million hectares) were owned by fewer than 2,000 landowners, as compared with 4.7 million acres (1.9 million hectares) farmed by 110,000 small farmers. Many large landowners do not live in Paraguay, and most farmers are squatters who supplement their income by working in trades and small business. Only a tiny minority of small farmers own the land on which they live and work.

Some attempts at land reform have been made. In 1963, the government created the Institute of Rural Welfare with a view to dividing up the large estates and distributing the land among the small farmers. Often, though, this has proved to be uneconomic either because the small plot cannot be made to work profitably, or because the small farmer has neither the capital nor the know-how to run his farm efficiently. As a result, the small plots are often left abandoned; and what was once part of a large productive estate lies fallow.

There is little sign of mechanization on the small farms, and oxen are still widely used. A typical scene, set against the wooded hills of eastern Paraguay, is of country people working with a yoke of oxen to press the juice from the sugarcane. Or, towards sunset, slowly disappearing down a country lane, the oxen pulling carts

A *carreta* (ox-drawn cart)—a typical sight in the Paraguayan countryside.

A family in rural Paraguay—most families are large, with several generations living under the same roof.

called *carretas* with oversize wheels for deep-rutted tracks and flooded areas, carrying cotton from the fields to the nearby market.

Many people in rural Paraguay still live in simple conditions, in huts of adobe brick and wood, without electricity or running water. They have few possessions and furniture is restricted to a few wooden essentials and hammocks. Cooking is on an open wood fire in a separate outhouse. A domed oven of mud brick may be used for baking the bread.

Families are usually large, with several generations living under one roof in conditions where disease can easily spread from one person to another. Pneumonia and infectious diseases are common causes of death. The average life expectancy has risen to 70 years in the past 10 years. A very high proportion of the population is under 30 years of age, even though there is a high rate of infant mortality.

The average Paraguayan farmer grows only what his family needs. The main crops are manioc and maize with rice, wheat, and sugarcane. In the neat plot that surrounds his hut, he will also have small plantations of *yerba maté*, coffee, tobacco, and a variety of fruits—particularly oranges and pineapples which are both native to Paraguay. Fruit is also taken from the Paraguayan coconut palm which grows wild across the eastern plain. Palm oil is extracted from the pulp of the fruit, coconut oil from the kernel, while the outer husk and inner shell surrounding the kernel may be used for fuel. Plantations of cultivated *Aleurites fordii* trees, covered in masses of white blossom in springtime, produce tung oil which is used in waterproofing cloth, varnishes, and soapmaking.

The most important cash crops for export are cotton and soybeans. Almost 95 percent of the annual cotton production is sold overseas—mainly to Europe and Japan. In 1996, cotton represented 21 percent of foreign income and soybeans 31 percent. In some years the export crops have been badly hit by rains and, in 1984, by the worst floods the country has known. It was a disaster for the economy with cotton and soybeans, which together make up 60 percent of Paraguay's earnings, dropping 20 percent below the expected figure. Also exported is petit-grain oil. This is distilled from the leaves of the bitter-orange tree for use in the perfume trade.

A Paraguayan farmer with his orange trees.

The export of *yerba maté* was once much greater than it is now, and today the demand is limited to South American countries. Although most country people grow their own supply of *yerba maté*, there are concentrations of the wild tree in the south, close to the border of Paraguay, Argentina, and Brazil. *Ilex paraguariensis*, the tree that produces *yerba maté*, grows to between 12 and 30 feet (three and a half and nine meters) high and is harvested between May and October when the leaves are mature. Most of the harvest for export is collected from these wild trees, said to have a better flavor than that of the cultivated trees, of which there are huge plantations in neighboring Argentina.

Paraguay is self-sufficient in most food, with the notable exception of wheat. Almost half the wheat needed has to be imported despite efforts to increase production. One region which is being

83

A wheatfield in southern Paraguay with "tung trees," covered in their distinctive white blossom, in the background.

developed for agriculture is in the southeast close to the Paraná River. Interestingly, it was this region which attracted the Jesuits three centuries ago. Instead of missions, the modern pioneers are building roads. Some of these, like the spectacularly engineered Route 6, cut through virgin forest. Unlike the tropical rain forest of the Amazon, the great forests of the Paraná are often cool and decomposition is slower, so a richer humus has formed beneath the trees. Paraguayan farmers, like their counterparts in Brazil across the river, have discovered the region's potential and are cutting giant swathes through the wilderness. Wheat and soybeans grow well on the fresh land and, because of the better humus, the annual yields can be sustained far longer than in the Amazon.

84

The newly opened-up land attracted settlers and, though it is still possible to travel almost 60 miles (100 kilometers) on Route 6 without seeing a house, both Encarnación in the south and Ciudad del Este in the north have expanded into the area.

Cattle were first introduced into Paraguay by the Spaniards and, in colonial times, large herds roamed the grasslands and forests. There were an estimated three million animals in 1800 but these herds were almost wiped out during the War of the Triple Alliance, and later in the Chaco War. To rebuild the herds, new stocks had to be brought from Brazil and Argentina. These included breeds like the Nelore and Brahmin which rear well on cattle *estancias* in the Chaco and on estates in other parts of the country. Tinned meat from Paraguay was in great demand during the Second World War. This gave the industry a boost and the number of cattle increased to around six million—a figure which has remained more or less stable ever since. Beef was a mainstay of the economy for a long time until, for various reasons, Paraguay was forced to scale down its export trade. This was because the establishment of the European Economic Community closed the European market. Paraguay was then faced with strong competition from other South American countries for the remaining world markets at a time when the price for beef was changing. Tinned meat production also fell and by 1981, the country's six meat-packing plants had been closed.

Another valuable export earner has been timber, though it has been decreasing in recent years forcing many sawmills to close. It has been estimated that over 30 percent of Paraguay is covered in

85

A small cattle farm in eastern Paraguay. Cattle were first introduced into Paraguay by the Spaniards in colonial times.

forest, although the extent of forest resources in the Chaco region has never been fully evaluated. Commercially the most valuable tree is the *quebracho*, or axe breaker, which is native to the Chaco. This is a tree with red wood that provides an extract used in tanning but, after many years of exploitation, it is becoming increasingly difficult to find a plentiful supply. The forests of the eastern region contain tropical hardwoods like the *cedro*, a tropical mahogany, and others that are not so familiar, like the *curupay* and *lapacho*. These trees grow to between 50 and 70 feet (15 and 21 meters) high, are straight, without limbs and said to be so heavy "as to sink in water like iron." Extensively used in building, these superb hardwoods last a long time even when exposed alternately to tropical storms and brilliant sun. Paraguay's forests are also well supplied with medicinal plants, including cinchona which yields the drug quinine used in the treatment of malaria. The Guaraní Indians knew many of the forests' secrets and their tradition is followed by most Paraguayans today, even in modern Asunción.

Rivers throughout Paraguay contain hundreds of species of fish. Like its Amazonian neighbors to the north, Paraguay has yet to tap its rivers as a rich source of protein and there is no organized fishing industry. People catch only what they need to eat or sell in the local market. Dorado is a game fish which averages over 15 pounds (7 kilograms) in weight though occasionally it reaches almost 30 pounds (14 kilograms). Surubí, a whiskered catfish commonly two to three feet (60 to 90 centimeters) and sometimes as much as eight feet (two and a half meters) long, is even more popular. Other catfish are even larger, weighing over 300 pounds (130 kilograms).

With such a variety of fresh produce, it is not surprising that Paraguayan tables abound with country-style dishes. A typical weekend will find families and friends gathered for an *asado* (barbecue) when large cuts of beef are skewered on poles and set to roast before a pit filled with glowing charcoal. Once cooked, the meat is passed around and the guests carve as much as they can eat. Rice, mandioca, and the tender hearts from the sprouts at the top of certain palms may be added to the meal. Bread may be made of wheat flour. Somewhat richer are the *chipas* made with maize flour and flavored with egg and cheese. *Chipa* stalls in the streets are part of the Paraguayan tradition and the women who run them—known as *chiperas*—offer snacks at a modest price.

Chipas—a type of bread made with maize flour and flavored with egg and cheese.

In the sugarcane districts especially, roadside shops and stalls serve a refreshing drink of chilled sugarcane juice or *mosto*, freshly pressed and served undiluted. The same juice is used on a larger scale to produce brown sugar. The liquid is boiled for several hours to evaporate the water. Once reduced, the liquid is poured into shallow pans and allowed to set as hard, brown blocks. The sugar can be used in this state or refined by other processes. Apart from the farmers' time, this crude sugar costs little to produce. The mill or press is driven by oxen and the fire below the boiling pan is fueled with the crushed, dry cane from which the juice has been extracted. In a more advanced energy-conscious scheme, Paraguay is also turning to cane sugar as the basis for alcohol to replace gas in motor vehicles. When developed it will become a truly renewable resource.

Soon, much of the old traditional Paraguay will be gone. A great deal is about to change in Paraguay affecting the agricultural lifestyle that has been followed for so many years. The country is on the verge of becoming an industrial nation, thanks to the power of its mighty rivers. For the first time, the energy in these limitless waters is being harnessed to provide cheap power, and a revolutionary transformation has already begun.

8

An Industrial Future?

Until recently, Paraguay was one of the least industrialized countries in South America. There are few developed mineral resources because most of the ore deposits are in remote locations. Two copper ores, malachite and azurite, are found near Caapucé. Gypsum and limestone are mined near the Paraguay River, and manganese has been located as well as marble, iron, and salt. Manufacturing industries have been limited to meat and timber processing, textiles, sugar, and extraction plants for *quebracho*, petit-grain, and vegetable oils. These industries have been centered in Asunción or at the location of the raw materials. Another source of income has been in black market trading, or contraband. Goods, particularly luxury items, are imported into the country with few taxes being paid, and then re-exported for sale in other Latin American countries. It has been and still is a very lucrative business, to which the government turns a blind eye. At times it has even been the mainstay of Paraguay's economy.

The country has industrialized somewhat and manufacturing

has come to account for almost one-quarter of the country's total production. From being one of the poorest countries in the Americas, Paraguay grew quickly in the mid-1900s and now has an annual growth rate of about 3 percent. Although accurate statistics are always hard to find, it is estimated that the average income per head of population had increased from U.S. $260 in 1970 to U.S. $3,900 in 1997, but this growth has stagnated recently.

One reason why Paraguay has been slow to develop industrially has been a lack of energy. Paraguay was dependent on wood-burning fuel to produce electrical energy. It was only with the completion of a hydroelectric dam on a tributary of the Paraná in 1968 that part of the country was electrified. The towns of Encarnación and Itauguá had lights for the first time in 1971 and Caacupé and Yaguarón in 1972. Paraguay's production of hydroelectric power increased 15-fold from 1970 to 1990.

The Paraná, which rises in the highlands of central Brazil, is 2,450 miles (3,943 kilometers) long, making it the second largest river of South America after the Amazon. Paraguay is fortunate to share the river with Brazil and Argentina, as both her large neighbors have an urgent need to increase their power supply. Paraguay made an agreement with Argentina to build another hydroelectric dam on the Paraná at Yacyretá and it was completed in the mid-1990s. As early as 1966 Paraguay and Brazil were discussing the possibility of a joint hydroelectric project on the Paraná. With a population of over 170 million, Brazil had seen its energy needs increase by an average of 10 percent annually for

The wood-fired kiln of a tile factory near Encarnación. Until the 1980s Paraguay was wholly dependent on wood as fuel.

some years; and in 1973 the two countries agreed to form the Itaipú Binational Company to administer an extraordinary dam.

The Itaipú Dam was constructed in seven years and is one of the largest hydroelectric dams in the world. When its full compliment of 18 turbines was installed in the early 1990s, it generated 12,600 megawatts. This compares with the world's previously biggest dam, the Grand Coulee in the United States, which produces only three-quarters of that amount of energy. Everything about Itaipú is massive. The main concrete dam is 623 feet (190 meters) high. This makes it almost three feet (one meter) higher than the National Westminster Tower in the city of London, Britain's tallest building, and half the height of the Empire State Building in New York. According to one estimate, 20.4 million cubic yards (15.6 million cubic meters) of concrete were used in its construction—enough to build all the structures in a city of four million people. The power house is almost over half a mile (1,000 meters) long, and here are the turbine generators, the largest ever made and each weighing over 3,000 tons.

When the dam was finished in 1982, a reservoir was created that covered an area of 564 square miles (1,460 square kilometers) of farmland and forests. The 30,000 inhabitants of the area, most of whom were farmers, were resettled. Conscious that the area was rich in wildlife, every effort was made to protect the monkeys, reptiles, and other animals by moving them to wildlife reserves in Brazil and other parts of Paraguay. But the creation of

The Itaipú Dam on the Paraná River. Built jointly by Paraguay and Brazil, this is one of the largest hydroelectric dams in the world.

the dam meant the disappearance of the Salto de Guairá waterfalls on the Paraná 127 miles (203 kilometers) to the north. The Guairá Falls (or the *Sete Quedas*, as they were known in Brazil) were much less well-known than the nearby spectacular Iguazu Falls but were, in terms of volume of water, the largest in the world and eight times larger than Niagara.

The cost of Itaipú has been estimated at 18 billion dollars. The project was financed mainly by Brazil with the help of international banks. Brazil also supplied specialized engineering expertise, while Paraguay contributed engineers and labor. The arrangement is that each country will receive 50 percent of the energy produced: in other words, each country will own nine of the turbine-generators. As Paraguay needs only about 5 percent of Itaipú's projected output for its own use, it will sell the surplus back to Brazil. Paraguay has received considerable funds in connection with the project. These had an immediate impact, particularly on the region closest to the dam. With the addition of the Yacyretá plant in the mid-1990s Paraguay is expected to become the world's largest exporter of electricity.

The Itaipú Dam is situated just eight miles (14 kilometers) from Friendship Bridge at Ciudad del Este. During the construction, 15,000 Paraguayan workers (who, together with their Brazilian counterparts, made up a workforce of 40,000) were employed on a 24-hour basis to complete the project on schedule. Three cement plants were built near the site to supply the enormous amount of concrete needed for the construction of the dam and estates of houses for the workers alongside the river bank. The Itaipú

The Guaira Falls (or *Sete Quedas*, as they were known in Brazil), which disappeared with the completion of the Itaipú Dam. In terms of volume of water, these were the largest in the world.

Binational Company undertook to provide the workers and their families with adequate living conditions, so that all had running water and electricity. Kitchens specially created for the site could feed 10,000 people at a sitting. Additionally, each neighborhood had paved streets, schools, churches, and medical facilities. Unemployment became a thing of the past. The one-time small river port became a boom town and then a city, complete with country club and golf course. The population of Ciudad del Este grew from 15,000 to almost 100,000 in the seven years of the dam's construction. Among the immediate improvements in the town were a water treatment plant, its first fire station, and a small airport.

As well as having had an immediate impact with the economic

95

spin-off from the construction work, Itaipú has enabled electrification work to be carried out in rural areas. Many country villages now have street lighting; and even in places where roadside lights would never be expected there are rows of concrete posts bearing new lamps. By working on Sundays the village communities erected their own lamps, just waiting for the day when the power line from the dam would reach them.

Funds have also been received in connection with the hydroelectric projects arranged with Argentina, although these projects have been delayed. The Yacyretá scheme is centered on the town of Encarnación. Encarnación is a busy port, connected by an elegant road bridge to the Argentine town of Posadas. It exports the timber, soybeans, *maté,* and cowhides of the region. The town has grown with the general trend of development in the region. The old center was close to the Paraná River and slightly above the seasonal high water level. A new center was built well above the Paraná for when the Yacyretá project was completed. A broad four-lane road leads from the riverside into the new city, and is connected to the auto routes leading northwest to Asunción and northeast to Ciudad del Este. Like all of Paraguay's principal border towns, Encarnación is serviced well by banks, many of them international, such as Lloyds and Citibank, and telecommunications are everywhere of the highest quality. The port itself is an Aladdin's cave of duty-free goods.

Other tangible developments brought about by the influx of foreign capital include the improved roads, both in the east of the country and across the Chaco. The route along the Paraná has

The Paraná River at Encarnación. The Argentine town of Posadas can be seen in the background on the other side of the river.

opened up areas which previously took days to reach or were totally isolated after heavy rain. The major Route 2, east from Asunción to the Paraná, was turned into a broad super-highway. Named Mariscal J. F. Estigarribia Highway, after the hero of the Chaco War, the road heads through the low, wooded hills surrounding Asunción, across rich farmland to the town of Coronel Oviedo. The next section to Ciudad del Este is Route 7 and is named after Dr. Francia, the first president of Paraguay. The route through the Chaco is paved for more than 300 miles (over 500 kilometers), and the last section of road is close to the Bolivian border.

Roads are also being improved in other parts of the country, though the pace is slower. Minor roads are still little more than hardened earth tracks which traffic soon churns into thick mud in the rain, and often vehicles cannot move until the surface has had time to dry.

The next few years will be a telling time in Paraguay's history. Clearly the republic does not have the resources to become a major industrial nation, but the sale of energy for foreign currency should assist investment and expansion in the country's agricultural economy. Given political stability and a degree of good luck, Paraguay's future is likely to be much brighter than that of most developing nations.

Construction work on the Trans Chaco Highway, opened up a previously unexploited and isolated area of the country.

GLOSSARY

asado	Barbecue where large cuts of beef are skewered on poles and roasted over a pit filled with hot charcoal
Asunceros	People of the city of Asunción
bottle dance	One of the folk dances of Paraguay in which a woman balances bottles on her head as she sways to the music
camelotes	Floating islands of water hyacinths seen on the Paraguay River when it floods
carreta	Carts with large oversize wheels pulled by oxen
cinchona	Plant from which the drug quinine is extracted for treatment of malaria
estancias	Large farms
matés	Vessels made from cow horns or vegetable gourds used to drink yerba maté tea
mestizo	Racial mixture of Spanish and Indian
mosto	Drink made from sugarcane juice

Nanduti lace	A delicate handmade lace that resembles a spider's web, woven by Paraguayan women into many designs
pampa	Large grass-covered plain
quebracho	A tree with wood so hard its name means axe-breaker. It provides an extract used in tanning
yerba maté	An herbal tea popular in Paraguay

INDEX